Polar Regions

Barbara James

Wayland

Our Green World

Acid Rain
Atmosphere
Deserts
Farming
Oceans
Polar Regions
Rainforests
Recycling
Wildlife

Cover: Polar bears on floating pack ice in the Arctic.

Book editor: Hazel Songhurst
Series editor: Philippa Smith
Series designer: Malcolm Walker

First published in 1992 by
Wayland (Publishers) Ltd
61 Western Road, Hove
East Sussex BN3 1JD, England

British Library Cataloguing in Publication Data
James, Barbara
Polar Regions. – (Our green world)
I. Title II. Series
333.73

HARDBACK ISBN 0-7502-0305-6

PAPERBACK ISBN 0-7502-0862-7

Typeset by Kudos Editorial and Design Services, Sussex, England
Printed in Italy by G. Canale & C.S.p.A., Turin

Contents

Words printed in **bold** in the main text are explained
in the glossary on page 45.

Poles apart

The two polar regions are among the wildest and coldest places on Earth. They have long, dark, freezing winters with no daylight. In the summer there is no night and the sun shines on the snow and ice from clear blue skies.

▲ *Penguins cannot fly but are superb swimmers.*

▲ *Autumn colours on the **tundra** in the Canadian Arctic.*

Where are the polar regions? They are at opposite ends of the planet, the Arctic in the north and the Antarctic in the south. Look at a map of the world, or a globe. You will find the North Pole at the top and South Pole at the bottom.

The Arctic

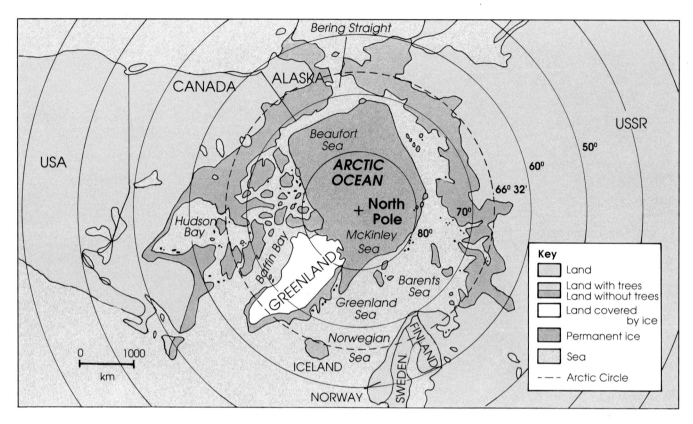

The centre of the Arctic is an ice cap, a huge block of ice that never melts. Around it is floating **pack ice**, **icebergs** and hundreds of islands, including Greenland, the world's largest island.

◀ *Freezing sea and icebergs along the coast of Greenland.*

The Arctic also includes the northern parts of North America, Europe and the USSR. The flat land is called tundra. Each summer, melting snow and ice form lakes and bogs here. The lowest temperature ever recorded in the Arctic is –68 °C.

▼ *The tundra is home to many animals and plants.*

The Antarctic

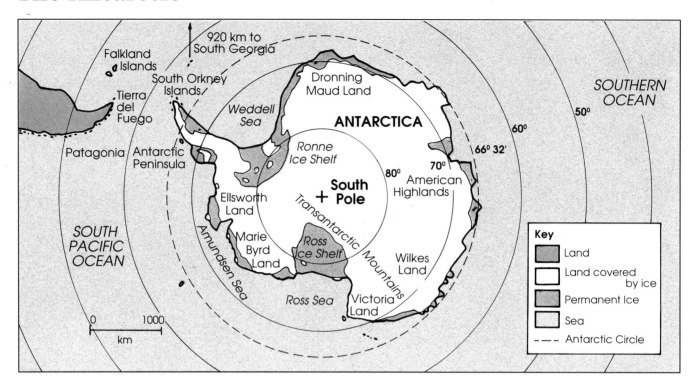

Antarctica is twice as big as Europe or Australia. It has high mountains and the land is covered by a thick ice sheet. On the oceans float huge blocks of ice called **ice shelves**.

▼ *Nine-tenths of an iceberg is hidden under the water.*

◀ *Two scientists studying plant life in the Antarctic.*

The Antarctic is the coldest place on Earth, where winter temperatures as low as −89 °C have been measured. There are roaring winds up to 160 kph but very little rain or snowfall – even less than in the Sahara Desert.

Why are the poles cold?

Look at the diagram. Because the Earth is round the sunlight at the poles spreads over a wider area than the sunlight that shines on the Equator. Also the thicker band of air at the poles makes it harder for the sun's heat to reach the land.

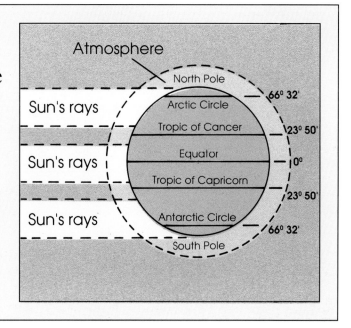

Atmosphere
North Pole
Sun's rays
Arctic Circle — 66° 32'
Tropic of Cancer — 23° 50'
Equator — 0°
Sun's rays
Tropic of Capricorn — 23° 50'
Antarctic Circle — 66° 32'
Sun's rays
South Pole

Differences between the Arctic and the Antarctic

	Arctic	Antarctic
1	Ocean surrounded by land	Land surrounded by ocean
2	Daylight months are March to September	Daylight months are September to March
3	Many ice-free areas	Very little ice-free land
4	Native peoples	No native peoples
5	Land belongs to countries such as Canada and the Soviet Union	Land belongs to no one
6	**Mining** for oil, gas	Mining is banned
7	Many **military bases**	Land set aside for peaceful purposes
8	Lots of **tourists**	Not many tourists

People have changed most places in the world, but the poles have always been difficult places for people to live because of the weather.

There are no big towns or cities at the poles. This is why they are still wild areas or **wilderness**.

▲ *Frozen trees and lakes in the Arctic in Finland.*

The polar regions are rich in wildlife. The Antarctic has fewer types (**species**) of animals and plants than the Arctic. Only the Antarctic has penguins and only the Arctic has polar bears.

In the Antarctic the freezing weather means few plants can grow. **Lichens** grow on patches of bare rock and provide a home (**habitat**) for insects. In the oceans there are millions of **microscopic** animals and plants called plankton floating near the surface.

▲ *Toadstools and moss growing on an Antarctic island.*

▲ ***Krill** are food for many Antarctic animals.*

The commonest Antarctic animal is the crabeater seal. Crabeaters, despite their name, feed on krill. The most famous Antarctic birds are penguins. There are seven species found in Antarctica.

A tiny Emperor penguin chick keeps warm. ▶

▲ *Huge male elephant seals fight on the sea ice.*

In the Arctic, the tundra is cold and snow-covered in winter, but in summer there are over 500 different wild flowers. They attract insects such as butterflies and wasps. The lakes and bogs are home for millions of mosquitoes. Many animals, such as **caribou**, move north (migrate) in the summer to feed. On the ground live voles, lemmings, foxes, hares and polar bears. In the sea are seals, walruses and whales.

▲ *This Arctic bramble is food for insects, birds and* **mammals**.

▲ *The Arctic poppy can be found on bare, rocky ground.*

The red-necked phalarope is a summer visitor to the Arctic. ▶

▼ *A lynx chases a hare.*

Animals and plants have to find a way to survive the weather at the poles. Most birds avoid the winter by moving south to warmer regions. Some animals, including polar bears, Arctic foxes and some Antarctic penguins stay through the winter. They have thick fur or fat to keep them warm.

▼ *These Arctic musk oxen have thick, furry coats to keep them warm.*

An Arctic fritillary butterfly. ▶

▼ *Wandering albatrosses nest in the Antarctic.*

The polar land can be easily damaged. Arctic plants grow very slowly and land damaged by vehicles or people may take many years to recover. The Arctic and Antarctic lands and oceans can also be badly affected by **pollution**, mining and tourists.

◄ *If the Arctic tundra is damaged, animals like this Arctic fox could lose their food supply.*

Rare calypso orchids. ▶

▲ *Two polar bears on the sea ice in Canada.*

Protecting polar bears

The polar bear is the largest meat-eating land animal.
It lives in the Arctic and feeds mainly on seals. In the 1960s
numbers of this beautiful white bear were falling. They were
hunted by people and their habitats were being lost to oil
and mine workings.

Six countries, Canada, Denmark, Greenland, Norway, the
USA and the USSR, have agreed to protect the bears. They
have stopped the hunting and protected the bears' habitats
and **migration** routes.

People at the poles

◄ *An Inuk (an Inuit man) prepares his sledge and husky dogs for a trip across the Greenland ice.*

Who lives at the poles? The Arctic has groups of native people whose families have lived there for hundreds of years. There are also people who have moved north to work in the oil and mining industries. In the Antarctic there are no native people. There are only scientists working at **research stations**.

The largest group of native people, the Inuit, live in the North American Arctic. In the past they hunted and trapped fish, seals and whales for food and clothing. Today, the Inuit still hunt but they also have modern lives. They have supermarkets, computers, snow vehicles and schools.

Hunting seals

Selling seal furs became a big industry for Arctic peoples. They sold the furs to people in Europe and North America.

However, **conservationists** argued against the killing of the seals. Now the American government and **European Community** (EC) have banned all seal products.

Many Arctic people have lost their jobs because of the ban.

▲ *The Inuit have always hunted sea mammals for food and fur.*

A Greenpeace member sprays a seal's fur with dye. This makes the fur useless to fur hunters. ▶

Most people think of the polar regions as harsh and unpleasant places. The Inuit and other native peoples have lived in the Arctic for **centuries**. They know how to **survive** there. They live in peace with their polar world. It is their home and they love it.

▼ *The Inuit live in modern houses, but they still build igloos like this when they are away on hunting trips.*

▲ *Modern technology is part of everyday life for Arctic peoples.*

Both the Arctic and the Antarctic have scientific research stations. The scientists study the polar animals and plants, rocks and soil, and weather. The conservation group Greenpeace has its own research station in Antarctica. It also checks that the other bases do not damage the polar **environment**.

Polar pollution

Although the poles are at the ends of the Earth, they have not escaped from pollution. Waste chemical gases are pumped into the air from factories and vehicle exhausts in other countries. The polluted air is blown around the world by winds. In the Arctic, pollution has changed the colour of the sky. This is called Arctic haze.

▲ *This paper mill in the USSR adds to pollution in the Arctic. But paper is wanted by millions of people.*

◀ *Scientists have found acid rain pollution in Arctic rivers and lakes.*

▲ *Lapland people depend on reindeer for their living.*
The Chernobyl explosion has changed their way of life.

Waste gases from other countries are also causing **acid rain** pollution. This is when the air pollution drops to Earth in the rain or snow. Some Arctic lakes have become so acid that fish and insects cannot live in them.

On 25 April 1986 there was a huge explosion at the Chernobyl nuclear power station in the USSR. It sent a **radioactive** pollution cloud into the air. The cloud drifted across Europe to the Arctic. The reindeer that live on the tundra have become poisoned and thousands have had to be killed.

The oceans have become the dustbin for a lot of human waste, such as factory chemicals and farm waste. Some chemicals are very poisonous, and when they reach the sea they can harm ocean creatures. Scientists have found that Arctic polar bears, living thousands of kilometres from a factory, have chemicals in their bodies.

Oil spills also pollute the oceans. In 1989, a supply ship sank in Antarctica. It caused an oil slick which killed penguins and other seabirds and huge numbers of krill. It may take 100 years for the area to return to normal.

▼ *Many creatures in the Antarctic feed on krill.*

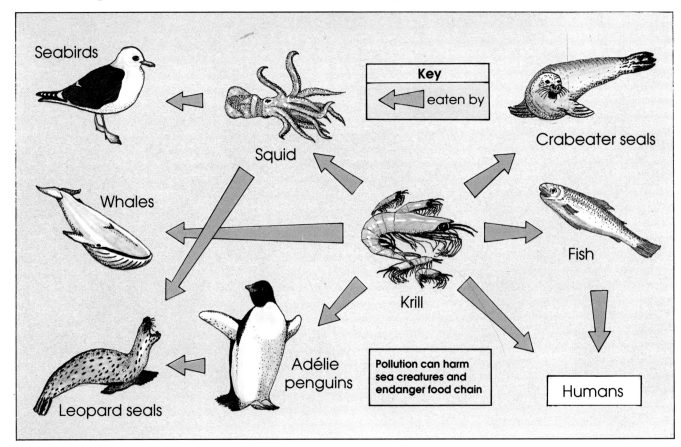

Seabirds

Squid

Key
⬅ eaten by

Crabeater seals

Whales

Fish

Krill

Adélie penguins

Pollution can harm sea creatures and endanger food chain

Humans

Leopard seals

◀ *Antarctic scientists check seawater underneath the ice for signs of pollution.*

Rubbish dumps

Once, the Arctic peoples threw nothing away and waste was eaten by dogs and Arctic foxes. Today, their lifestyle has changed and all kinds of rubbish is found on frozen dumps.

A rubbish dump in the Canadian Arctic. ▶

Weather at the poles

People and governments around the world are concerned about the greenhouse effect, or global warming. What is the greenhouse effect?

The Earth is covered by a blanket of gases called the **atmosphere**. The atmosphere contains 'greenhouse gases' such as carbon dioxide, methane and ozone. The sun warms the Earth and gradually the heat escapes back into space. The greenhouse gases act like a greenhouse by trapping some of the sun's heat.

▼ *Global warming could melt parts of the polar ice caps.*

Without the greenhouse effect the Earth would be too cold for any life. However, the delicate balance of gases in the atmosphere is changing.

People today burn huge amounts of fuel. This increases the amount of greenhouse gases in the atmosphere. This means more heat is trapped, so the Earth is getting warmer. Scientists think this might cause parts of the polar ice caps to melt. Then sea levels would rise around the world, causing flooding.

One way of reducing global warming is to burn less fuel. Water power is one way electricity can be made without burning fuel.

This dam uses water power to produce electricity. ▶

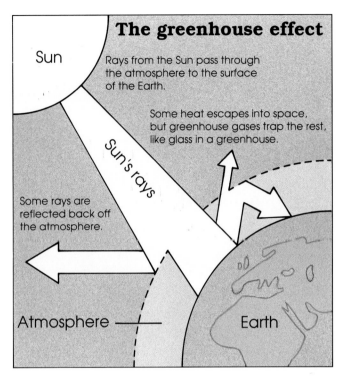

The greenhouse effect

Sun

Rays from the Sun pass through the atmosphere to the surface of the Earth.

Some heat escapes into space, but greenhouse gases trap the rest, like glass in a greenhouse.

Sun's rays

Some rays are reflected back off the atmosphere.

Atmosphere ——

Earth

Ozone is an important gas in the atmosphere because it protects the Earth from the sun's harmful ultraviolet (UV) rays. Scientists in the Antarctic found a hole in the ozone layer. If more UV rays reach the Earth they could harm life on Earth.

▲ Scientists at this research station in the Canadian Arctic check the world's weather.

When two oxygen atoms join together it forms the oxygen we breathe. When a third oxygen atom comes along, it forms ozone.

1.

One oxygen atom

2 joined oxygen atoms

Ozone

2.

Chlorine

Ozone

The ozone is destroyed

When a chlorine atom from CFCs collides with ozone, it steals one of the atoms and the ozone is destroyed.

◄ This diagram shows how CFCs destroy the ozone in the atmosphere.

The ozone hole is caused by chemicals called CFCs (chlorofluorocarbons). They are used in the cooling systems of fridges, in foam packaging and in some aerosol cans. Many countries have agreed to stop using CFCs but it will take many years for the ozone layer to return to normal.

An icy museum

The polar ice contains a record of its history. Scientists drill deep into the polar ice sheets and remove a core of ice. The ice core shows changes in weather over many years. It also shows how much pollution has been in the air.

Scientists drill into the ice cap to remove an ice core. ▶

Polar treasure chests

The Arctic has vast stores of **minerals** such as oil, gas, coal, copper and gold. To obtain the minerals people have built huge mines, drilling rigs, pipelines and tanker terminals. The industry brings money and jobs to these areas. But it also brings pollution and destroys wildlife habitats.

In the Antarctic, minerals have been discovered but they have not been mined. This is because the Antarctic Treaty, an international agreement, forbids any mining.

◀ *Miners in Arctic Sweden.*

▲ *Alaska supplies much of North America's oil and gas.*

The Trans-Alaska Pipeline

The Trans-Alaska oil pipeline stretches 1300 km across Alaska. It took three years to build and crosses mountains, tundra and forest.

In several places, the pipeline was moved to avoid important wildlife areas and bird nesting sites. In other places it was raised so that large animals, such as caribou, could walk underneath it.

The Trans-Alaska Pipeline carries oil across Alaska to the coast, where tankers take it to the USA and Europe. ▶

In March 1989, Alaska suffered the worst ever oil spill in American waters. The tanker, *Exxon Valdez*, ran aground spilling 35,000 tonnes of oil. Shorelines were covered with oil and thousands of fish, birds and sea mammals were killed. It took months to clean it up.

▼ *Cleaning the shore after the* Exxon Valdez *oil spill.*

An Antarctic research station. ▶

▼ *A brown bear catches a salmon. Animals like this were affected by the Exxon Valdez oil spill.*

The polar regions have large numbers of fish, seals, whales and krill. The Arctic produces one-tenth of the world's fish catch. Arctic peoples have always eaten food from the sea. Today there are also big fishing fleets from other countries such as the USSR and Japan. These fleets catch huge amounts of fish. As a result, some fish species have become low in numbers.

▲ *Fish is an important food for many people in the world.*

▲ *A whaling ship. Many countries have now stopped killing whales.*

Overfishing has also happened in the Antarctic. Now an international fishing agreement has been signed to stop fishermen taking too many fish.

In the Antarctic, there is a small but growing tourist industry. The visitors go to watch the wildlife. The Arctic is easier to reach and so there are more tourists there. They go on wildlife tours and hunting trips.

▼ *In Greenland, the money that tourists spend helps local villages.*

▼ *Tourists in the Arctic watch a wild polar bear.*

By visiting these beautiful wild places, people understand more about them and the need to protect them. Tourism also brings money to the areas. However, tourists can disturb the wildlife they come to see.

▼ *A tourist cruise ship in the Antarctic.*

Protecting the poles

Who owns the polar regions? The Arctic lands and seas belong to different countries who can use the land as they wish. The USSR and USA see the Arctic as an important area and they have military bases there.

The Antarctic belongs to no one. The region is covered by an international agreement called the Antarctic Treaty. It says that Antarctica is for 'scientific research in the interest of all mankind' and that it must be used only for peaceful purposes. This means it cannot be mined or developed in any way. It must be left as wilderness.

▲ *Flags of some of the countries that have signed the Antarctic Treaty.*

▲ *An ice-breaker ship delivers supplies to the British base in Antarctica.*

However some countries want to use the oil, gas, metals and other riches that are underneath the Antarctic ice. They do not want to renew the Treaty. The future of Antarctica is uncertain.

▲ *In 1989 Greenpeace campaigners protested against French plans to build an airstrip in Antarctica.*

In 1972, conservationists called on world governments to make Antarctica a World Park. The World Park would protect Antarctica's wilderness forever. Mining, military bases and waste dumping would be banned. The World Park cannot be set up until it is supported by most countries in the world.

The polar regions are beautiful lands. We need to protect these special areas and the animals, plants and peoples living there. The poles also need to be protected because they help balance world weather systems.

▼ *Two moose bulls in an Alaskan National Park.*

The Arctic

The first person to reach the North Pole was the American Robert E. Peary in 1909.

The Antarctic

In 1911, Roald Amundsen of Norway became the first person to reach the South Pole.

How you can help

1 Support organizations working to protect the poles, such as Greenpeace.
2 Learn more about the poles and tell your friends.
3 Look for the 'ozone friendly' label if you buy aerosol cans.
4 Slow down the greenhouse effect by using less energy. Switch off lights and heaters when they are not needed.

What does the future hold for the Inuit of the Arctic? ▶

Glossary

Acid rain   Rain, snow and mist that has become acid from pollution.

Atmosphere   The layer of gases surrounding the Earth.

Caribou   A type of deer found in the North American Arctic.

Centuries   One century is 100 years.

Conservationists   People who want to protect our world and its wildlife from harm.

Environment   A plant's or animal's surroundings including air, water, soil and rocks.

European Community (EC)   A group of European countries which work together.

Habitat   The area in which plants and animals live, such as a woodland, desert or rock pool.

Icebergs   Huge pieces of floating ice.

Ice shelves   Huge thicknesses of ice attached to land but spreading out over the sea.

Krill   Very tiny shrimp-like animals. They are food for millions of fish, birds and sea mammals, such as seals and whales.

Lichens   Non-flowering plants.

Mammals   Warm-blooded animals, such as polar bears and humans. The females feed their young on their own milk.

Microscopic   Used to describe something so tiny that it can only be seen using a microscope.

Migration   The movement of animals from one region to another at different times of the year.

Military bases   Army, air force or navy bases.

Minerals   Substances such as coal and tin, formed naturally in rocks and soil.

Mining The process of taking minerals from the ground.

Pack ice A large area of floating ice.

Pollution Harmful substances such as rubbish, factory smoke and poisonous wastes that damage the environment.

Radioactive Used to describe radioactivity, a kind of energy which can damage living things.

Research stations Places where scientists study.

Species A set of animals or plants that can be grouped together.

Survive To stay alive in spite of difficult conditions.

Tourists People on holiday, or who are travelling for pleasure.

Tundra A polar environment, usually flat and treeless with low shrubs, mosses and lichens.

Wilderness A wild area where no humans live.

Picture acknowledgements
Bryan and Cherry Alexander *cover*, 6, 13 below, 14 right, 16 below, 19, 20, 21 above, 22, 23, 24 above, 25, 27 below, 30, 32, 33, 37, 38 left, 44; British Antarctic Survey 9, 12 left (R Lewis-Smith), 40 (C W M Swithinbank); Bruce Coleman Ltd 5, 18 right (B & C Calhoun), 7 (Charlie Ott), 11 (Norbert Rosing), 12 right (Inigo Everson), 14 left (Pekka Helo), 15 above (Konrad Wothe), 16 above, 35 below (Eckart Pott), 39 (Jen and Des Bartlett); GeoScience Features 24; Greenpeace 21 below, 42; Oxford Scientific Films 13 above (Doug Allan), 17, 28, 35 (Ben Osborne), 27 above (Kim Westerskov), 31 (Stephen Mills), 36 (Doug Allan), 43 (Frank Huber); Rex Features 34 (J Schultz); ZEFA 4, 8 (K Graham), 15 below, 18 left, 29 (Slatter), 38 right (Sunak). The illustrations are by Marilyn Clay.

Finding out more

Books to read

The Arctic and the Antarctic by Cass Sandak (Franklin Watts, 1987)
Atmosphere by John Baines (Wayland, 1991)
Inuit by Anne Smith (Wayland, 1989)
Life in the Polar Lands by Monica Byles (Two-Can, 1990)
Polar Lands by Norman Barrett (Franklin Watts, 1991)
Seals and Sea Lions by V. Papastavrou (Wayland, 1991)

Useful addresses

Friends of the Earth (UK)
26-28 Underwood Street
London N1 7JQ

Greenpeace (New Zealand)
Private Bag
Wellesley Street
Auckland

Greenpeace (Australia)
310 Angas Street
Adelaide 5000

Greenpeace (UK)
Canonbury Villas
London N1 2PN

Greenpeace (Canada)
427 Bloor Street West
Toronto, Ontario

United Nations Environment
  Programme (UK)
c/o IIED
3 Endsleigh Street
London WC1H 0DD

World Wide Fund for Nature
International Education
  Division
1196 Gland, Switzerland

World Wide Fund for Nature (UK)
Panda House
Weyside Park
Godalming
Surrey GU7 1XR

Index